Recipes for
Art and Craft Materials

Recipes for Art and Craft Materials

Written and illustrated by

Helen Roney Sattler

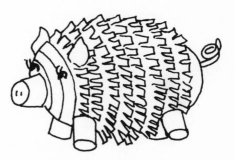

Lothrop, Lee & Shepard Company / New York

Books by Helen Roney Sattler

Recipes for Art and Craft Materials
Jewelry From Junk
Sock Craft: *Toys, Gifts, and Other Things to Make*
Kitchen Carton Crafts
Holiday Gifts, Favors, and Decorations That You Can Make

3   4   5   77   76   75   74

Sattler, Helen Roney.
    Recipes for art and craft materials.

    SUMMARY: Instructions for making pastes, modeling compounds, papier-mâché, paints, inks, and numerous other materials for art and craft work.
    1. Handicraft—Equipment and supplies—Juvenile literature. 2. Artists' materials—Formulae, tables, etc.—Juvenile literature. [1. Handicraft—Equipment and supplies. 2. Artists' materials] I. Title.
TT153.7.S27   745.5′028   73-4950
ISBN 0-688-41557-1
ISBN 0-688-51557-6 (lib. bdg.)

to my family

Contents

Using This Book

There are fun and adventure in this book. With it, you can learn how to make your own materials for art projects. The most often used and asked for art and craft recipes are here. They will save classroom teachers and leaders of troops, campers, clubs, and church and temple groups much money and effort because so many different recipes are compiled under one cover. When children learn to mix and make their own materials, many avenues of creative expression can open up to them. Busy mothers will find many useful rainy-day projects that will both occupy and entertain children.

Most of the materials used in these recipes are inexpensive and are found in the home. A few items must be purchased in crafts stores or in pharmacies. In either case, the finished product will be less expensive than a ready-made product. It will certainly be more rewarding.

The first thing you should do is read the Helpful Hints section and look through the entire book to become acquainted with the various recipes in it. You will find several recipes for the same thing, such as paste, finger paint, and modeling compound. Some are simple, some are more complicated. Each is different in texture or consistency. You will have fun experimenting with different recipes to determine which you prefer.

Most of the recipes are designed and measured for individual projects. Some recipes include instructions on how to increase them for group work. Teachers, parents, and group leaders should read each one to determine which is best suited for their particular need.

Although an effort has been made to avoid the use of harmful ingredients, it is recommended that, when making these recipes, children be supervised to prevent accidents. It is also recommended that no one be allowed to eat or taste any of the finished products. They are not for human consumption.

Helpful Hints

1. There are many preservatives for pastes, finger paints, and modeling compounds. You can use alum, oil of cloves, oil of cinnamon, oil of wintergreen, oil of peppermint, pure denatured alcohol, sodium benzoate, and boric acid solution. In most cases only one or two of these are listed in the recipe. You can substitute any among the above for those listed in the recipe. The ones suggested in this book are those most frequently found in the home. Or they can be purchased at a pharmacy or at the drug counter of a grocery store. These substances should not be eaten. Boric acid solution is a weak solution used for eyewashes. Powdered alum is often used as a canker-sore remedy.

2. For the most part, coloring materials have been limited to poster paints, powdered pigments, dyes, food coloring, and zinc oxide because they are most readily available and least expensive. Zinc oxide powder is a paint pigment that is often used in antiseptic lotions. It can be purchased in a pharmacy.

3. Unless another kind is specifically called for, always use plain non-self-rising wheat flour in all recipes calling for flour.

4. For successful results, all measurements should be followed carefully. Since ingredients may vary somewhat from brand to brand, you may have to experiment until you have found the correct mixture.

5. Never pour leftover plaster or plaster mix down the drain. It will clog drainpipes.

6. A plastic coffee-can lid or similar plastic lid is a good base on which to model bowls or figures with modeling compounds. It can be easily turned so that you can work on all parts of the object, and you can easily carry it to another place for drying.

7. You may need to purchase a palette pan for mixing paints.

8. Dextrine, which is used in some of these recipes, is easily obtainable in most groceries or drugstores. It is a powdered or granulated sugar substitute. It usually contains saccharin, but this will not affect the recipe.

9. All of the other ingredients used in this book can be purchased in a grocery or a drugstore, except rosin, resin glue, and plaster of Paris; these items can be purchased at a lumberyard or hardware store.

10. In several recipes, commercial white household glue—a casein glue—is suggested for expedience. When other glues can be substituted, they are mentioned.

Pastes

Thin Paste

You Will Need:
  ¼ cup sugar
  ¼ cup non-self-rising wheat flour
  ½ teaspoon powdered alum
1¾ cups water
  ¼ teaspoon oil of wintergreen

How to Make It:
1. Mix sugar, flour, and alum together.
2. Gradually add 1 cup water, stirring vigorously to prevent lumps.
3. Boil until clear and smooth, stirring constantly.
4. Add remainder of water and oil of wintergreen. Stir until thoroughly mixed.

Makes 1 pint.

How to Use It: Spread with a brush or tongue depressor.
  Thin Paste is an excellent adhesive for scrapbooks, collages, and Strip Papier-mâché (page 62).
  It can be stored in a jar for several months without refrigeration.

Paper Paste

You Will Need:
⅓ cup non-self-rising wheat flour
2 tablespoons sugar
1 cup water
¼ teaspoon oil of peppermint or oil of wintergreen

How to Make It:
1. Mix flour and sugar. Gradually add water, stirring vigorously to prevent lumps.
2. Cook over low heat until clear, stirring constantly.
3. Remove from stove and add oil of peppermint or wintergreen. Stir until well blended.

Makes about 1 cup.

How to Use It: Spread with a brush or tongue depressor.

Soft, smooth, thick, and white, Paper Paste has a good spreading consistency and is especially appropriate for use with small children or for any paste-up work.

This paste can be stored in a covered jar for several weeks without refrigeration.

Transparent Library Paste

You Will Need:
- ¾ cup rice flour (can be purchased at health food store or diet food counter in grocery)
- 2 tablespoons sugar
- ¾ cup cold water
- 2½ cups boiling water
- ½ teaspoon oil of wintergreen

How to Make It:

1. Mix rice flour and sugar with cold water in a pan. Stir until smooth.

2. Add boiling water.

3. Bring to boil over low heat, stirring constantly, until mixture thickens.

4. Remove from heat and add oil of wintergreen.

Makes 1½ pints.

How to Use It: Spread with a brush or tongue depressor.

Transparent Library Paste is an excellent paste for mending books. Cut a piece of white tissue paper the size and shape of the tear. Spread paste over the tissue and lay the tissue over tear. It will be transparent when it dries.

You can use this paste for tissue-paper collage and scrapbooks.

If stored in a tightly sealed jar, it will keep for several months without refrigeration.

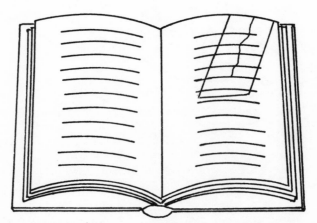

Classroom Paste

You Will Need:
- 1 cup non-self-rising wheat flour
- 1 cup sugar
- 1 cup cold water
- 4 cups boiling water
- 1 tablespoon powdered alum
- ½ teaspoon oil of wintergreen (optional)

How to Make It:

1. Mix flour and sugar. Slowly stir in cold water to form a paste.

2. Slowly add boiling water, stirring vigorously to prevent lumps.

3. Bring mixture to a boil, stirring constantly, until thick and clear.

4. Remove from heat and add alum. Stir until well mixed.

5. Add oil of wintergreen if paste is not to be used immediately.

Makes about 1½ quarts.

How to Use It: Classroom paste is a good all-purpose paste, especially appropriate for work with children. It is also excellent for papier-mâché projects.

Stored in a closely capped jar, it will keep for several weeks. It stores better than Paper Paste (page 17) and is a little softer. It can be thinned with hot water if it gets too thick for easy spreading.

Resin Papier-mâché Paste

You Will Need:
- ½ cup of non-self-rising wheat flour
- ¼ cup powdered resin glue
- ½ cup warm water
- 1½ cups hot water
- 4 drops oil of wintergreen

How to Make It:

1. Mix flour and resin glue in a saucepan.

2. Make a paste with a ½ cup of warm water. Add hot water, stirring vigorously to prevent lumps.

3. Cook over low heat, stirring constantly, until thick, clear, and smooth.

Makes about 1 pint.

How to Use It: For best results, use this paste within a few days of preparation.

It gives a very hard finish to papier-mâché projects and is excellent to use in making large permanent objects such as furniture, candlesticks, and bowls.

Wallpaper Paste

You Will Need:
- 4 cups non-self-rising wheat flour
- 1 cup sugar
- 1 gallon warm water
- 1 quart cold water
- ½ teaspoon oil of wintergreen or oil of cinnamon (optional)

How to Make It:
1. Mix flour and sugar in a saucepan.
2. Add enough warm water (a little at a time) to make a smooth paste. Then add the rest of the warm water slowly, stirring vigorously to prevent lumps.
3. Bring mixture to a boil, stirring constantly. Cook until thick and clear.
4. Thin with about 1 quart cold water to desired thickness.
5. Add oil of wintergreen or oil of cinnamon if paste is not to be used the same day it is made.

Makes about 1½ gallons.

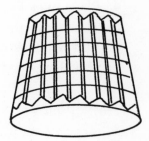

How to Use It: This paste spreads best when used warm. It will keep for a few days.

This is a good paste to use for Strip Papier-mâché (page 62) and other projects that require a large amount of paste. You can use it when covering lampshades and wastebaskets with cloth or wallpaper where durability is not required.

21

Paperhanger's Paste

You Will Need:
    1 cup non-self-rising wheat flour
    1 tablespoon powdered alum
    1 tablespoon powdered rosin
1½ cups warm water
4½ cups hot water
1½ cups cold water
    8 drops oil of wintergreen, oil of cloves, or oil of cinnamon
       (optional)

How to Make It:
1. Mix flour, alum, and rosin in a saucepan.
2. Make a paste by adding 1½ cups warm water. Stir until smooth.
3. Pour in 4½ cups hot water, stirring vigorously to prevent lumps.
4. Place over low heat and boil until thick and clear.
5. Thin with about 1½ cups cold water.
6. Add 8 drops of oil of wintergreen, cloves, or cinnamon as preservative if paste is not to be used the same day it is made.

Makes about 1½ quarts. Can be doubled for large projects.

How to Use It: This paste is best when used warm. As it cools, it will thicken. It can be thinned with more warm water. If preservative is added, it will keep several months. The recipe can be doubled or quadrupled for large projects.

Paperhanger's Paste can be used for papier-mâché projects when a hard finish is desired. Use this paste when a durable binder is needed, as when gluing cloth on cardboard to reinforce box corners or scrapbook hinges or similar projects.

Stamp Gum

You Will Need:
  1 packet (¼ ounce) unflavored gelatin
  1 tablespoon cold water
  3 tablespoons boiling water
  ½ teaspoon white corn syrup
  ½ teaspoon lemon or peppermint extract
  2 drops boric acid solution

How to Make It:
1. Sprinkle gelatin into cold water in a small bowl. Put aside until softened.
2. Pour softened gelatin into boiling water and stir until completely dissolved.
3. Add corn syrup, lemon or peppermint extract, and boric acid solution. Mix well.

Makes 4 ounces.

How to Use It: Brush thinly onto the back of a stamp. When dry, moisten the stamp and apply it to paper.

   This gum will gel overnight. To return it to a liquid state, warm it in a pan of hot water. It will keep several months if stored in a 4-ounce pill bottle.

Seal and Envelope Mucilage

You Will Need:
6 tablespoons pure white vinegar
4 packets (1 ounce) unflavored gelatin
1 tablespoon peppermint extract

How to Make It:
1. Bring vinegar to a boil. Add gelatin and stir until completely dissolved.
2. Add peppermint extract. Stir until well mixed.

Makes about ½ cup.

How to Use It: Use a brush to spread mucilage thinly on back of a label or an envelope flap. Dry. Moisten to apply.

This is a thicker, heavier glue than Stamp Gum (page 23). You can use this mucilage to adhere paper to paper or to cardboard. Apply and stick at once.

With this mucilage and paper, you can make your own envelopes, note stationery, labels, and seals. There is enough here for a large group project to use to make gifts or bazaar items. It makes enough to cover several dozen envelopes or labels.

Store leftover mucilage in a capped bottle. It will keep for several months without spoiling. It will set when cooled, however. To use again, melt by setting the bottle in a pan of warm water.

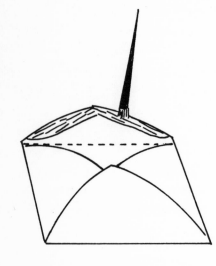

Mucilage

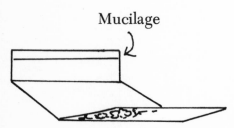

Waterproof or Glass Glue

You Will Need:
2 packets (½ ounce) unflavored gelatin
2 tablespoons cold water
3 tablespoons skimmed milk
  few drops oil of wintergreen (optional)

How to Make It:
1. In a small bowl, sprinkle gelatin over cold water. Set aside to soften.
2. Heat milk to boiling point and pour into softened gelatin. Stir until dissolved.
3. Add oil of wintergreen as preservative if glue is to be kept for more than a day.

Makes about ⅓ cup.

How to Use It: With a brush, apply a thin layer to the objects to be glued while the glue is still warm.

This is the best glue to use for projects in which glass must be adhered to glass. For glass jars, it is best to use the glue in its liquid state. For gluing marbles together or gluing metal ornaments to metal cans, use the glue in its gelled state. This glue is waterproof and can be used to mend china, to glue labels on home canned foods and jellies, or to glue wood to wood.

Store in a screw-capped jar. It will gel as it cools, but this will not affect its adhesiveness. Set jar in a pan of hot water to reuse.

25

Bookbinding or Leather Glue

You Will Need:
1 packet (¼ ounce) unflavored gelatin
3 tablespoons boiling water
1 tablespoon vinegar
1 teaspoon glycerine

How to Make It:
1. Add gelatin to boiling water. Stir until it is completely dissolved.
2. Add vinegar and glycerine. Stir until well mixed.

Makes about ⅓ cup. For larger projects, double the recipe.

How to Use It: Apply thinly with a brush while the glue is still warm.

This glue is excellent for binding leather to leather. When used on leather, it is waterproof. It also makes a good flexible glue for paper, or for gluing cloth to cardboard for notebook binders or scrapbooks.

Stored in a tightly capped plastic or glass jar, this glue will keep for several months. It will gel in the bottle after a few days. Warm in hot water to reuse.

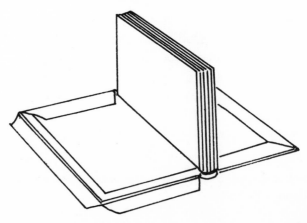

Collage or Découpage Glue

You Will Need:
3 parts white household glue *
1 part warm water

How to Make It:
1. Combine glue with water in a jar or a bottle with a screw-top lid.
2. Shake until well mixed.

How to Use It: To make a collage, brush a thin layer of glue to the back surface of the paper scraps or pictures and smooth onto a piece of cardboard.

In making découpage, cut out design and brush a thin layer of glue to the back surface. Lay the design onto surface to be decorated and smooth out all air bubbles and wrinkles.

This glue may be stored indefinitely.

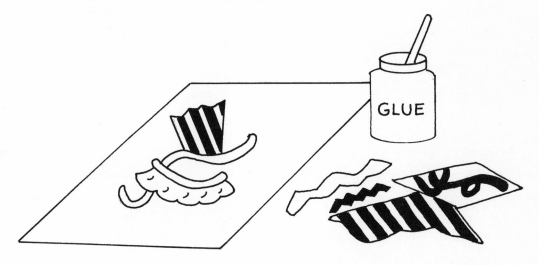

* A thin solution of Paperhanger's Paste (page 22) or Waterproof or Glass Glue (page 25) can be substituted.

Modeling Compounds

Preparing Natural Clay

You Will Need:
  natural clay
1 two-pound coffee can
  old newspapers
  a hammer or rock
¼-inch-mesh sieve
2 three-pound coffee cans with lids
  water
  window-screen wire
  large plaster bowls or cloth-lined bowls

How to Make It:

Many areas contain natural clay banks. These vary in color—gray, green, red, or yellow—depending upon the mineral found in combination with the clay. This natural clay can be used to make pottery or sculpture.

1. Select a clay deposit that is as free from impurities (sand, gravel, dirt, plant roots, and stems) as possible. Dig enough clay to fill a two-pound coffee can.

2. Spread the clay out on a newspaper and place it in the sun to dry completely.

3. The clay will dry in hard lumps. With a hammer or rock, break these lumps into a fine powder, but be careful not to crush pebbles or rock chips into the clay. These would add impurities.

4. Sift the powdered clay through the sieve. Throw away all pebbles.

5. Fill 1 three-pound coffee can ⅔ full

with the sifted clay. Completely cover clay with water. As the water soaks in, pour on more water so that the clay will remain covered.

6. Using your hands, stir the clay to evenly distribute the water throughout.

7. Soak for about 2 hours or until the mixture is the consistency of thick cream.

8. Pour this creamy mixture through a piece of window-screen wire into another coffee can or a bucket.

9. Let this strained mixture sit overnight, or until all the clay has settled to the bottom. Then pour off clear water that has accumulated on top. Do not stir up the thick "slip" underneath.

Plaster Bowl

10. Pour the remaining thick slip into large plaster bowls or bowls lined with dry cloths. Plaster bowls are best if you have them, but cloth-lined bowls are satisfactory. As the cloth absorbs the water, the slip stiffens and separates from the cloth or plaster. It is then ready to store in covered coffee cans for several days. The clay improves with age. You should store it wetter than you want it to work with, since the clay will dry out when you cut and wedge it.

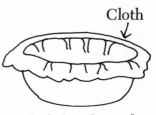

Cloth-lined Bowl

11. All clay must be "wedged" to remove the air bubbles from it before it can be used for bowl making or sculpting. Cut the clay into pieces and throw each piece with force against the table many times until you are sure no more air bubbles remain. After this is done your clay is the same as any that is commercially prepared. It is now ready to use.

If the clay will not hold its shape, you can improve it by adding a little fine sand.

If the clay crumbles at the edges when you press it between your fingers, it is too sandy. If the clay is too sandy to work with, there is little that can be done to improve it. It is best to discard it and select another clay deposit. With a little experimentation and practice you will soon learn which kind suits you best.

Quick and Easy
Modeling Dough

You Will Need:
¾ cup flour (use any kind except self-rising flour)
½ cup salt
1½ teaspoons powdered alum
1½ teaspoons vegetable oil
½ cup boiling water
food coloring

How to Make It:
1. Mix flour, salt, and alum in a mixing bowl.
2. Add vegetable oil and boiling water. Stir vigorously with a spoon until well blended. Dough should not stick to the sides of the bowl and should be cool enough to handle.
3. Add food coloring and knead into dough until color is well blended and the dough is the desired tint.

Makes about 1 cup. Double the recipe for large projects. For groups, mix several double recipes rather than one large amount.

How to Use It: This is an excellent play dough. It has a smooth texture, takes about 15 minutes to make, and dries to a hard finish overnight. You can make lovely dough flowers as well as animals and other figures with it.

Store in a jar with a tight lid. Dough will keep several months without refrigeration.

Play Clay

½ cup salt
½ cup hot water
¼ cup cold water
½ cup cornstarch

How to Make It:
1. Mix salt and hot water in a pan and bring to boiling point.
2. Stir cold water into cornstarch.
3. Add cornstarch mixture to boiling water. Stir vigorously to prevent lumps.
4. Cook over low heat, stirring constantly, until mixture is like stiff pie dough.
5. Remove from heat and turn out onto a breadboard to cool.
6. As soon as mixture is cool enough to handle, knead until smooth and pliable.

Makes about 1½ cups.

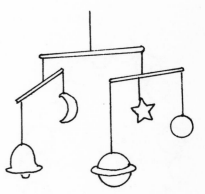

How to Use It: Play Clay has a grainy texture and is excellent for flattening with a rolling pin and cutting into shapes to make mobiles and Christmas tree decorations.

It dries and hardens in 1 to 2 days. When dry, it is white and can be painted with enamels. To speed up drying time, bake on a cookie sheet in an oven at 200 degrees F. for 1 hour.

Wrapped in aluminum foil or plastic or kept in a airtight container, it will keep a long time without refrigeration.

Cooked Salt and Flour Clay

You Will Need:
¾ cup salt

½ cup flour (use any kind except self-
    rising flour)

2 teaspoons powdered alum

¾ cup water

2 tablespoons vegetable oil
    food coloring

¼ cup non-self-rising wheat flour

How to Make It:
1. Mix salt, flour, and alum in a saucepan.

2. Add water slowly, stirring to prevent lumps.

3. Place over low heat, and cook, stirring constantly, until mixture is rubbery and difficult to stir. It should not be sticky when touched with your finger.

4. Add vegetable oil. Stir until blended.

5. Turn out onto a plate or aluminum foil. Set aside until cool enough to handle.

6. Divide mixture into portions and to each portion add a different food coloring if desired. Knead until color is blended.

7. Add ¼ cup flour if needed to prevent sticking.

Makes 1½ cups.

How to Use It: Model as with clay—especially good for making beads or pressing into molds. Hardens in 1 to 2 days; do not bake. Store in an airtight container.

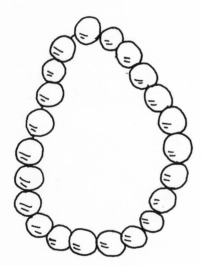

Play Dough

You Will Need:
2¼ cups non-self-rising wheat flour
  1 cup salt
  1 tablespoon powdered alum
  4 tablespoons vegetable oil
1½ cups boiling water
     food coloring or poster paints

How to Make It:
1. Mix flour, salt, and alum. Add vegetable oil.
2. Stir in boiling water. Stir vigorously with a large spoon until mixture holds together.
3. Knead the dough until it is smooth.
4. Divide the dough into several lumps. Add a few drops of food coloring or poster paint to each lump and knead to mix the color into the dough.

Makes about 3 cups.

How to Use It: Model as with clay. Objects will dry to a hard finish if left in the open air. Paint dried pieces with enamel, hyplar, or tempera.
    Stored in an airtight container, Play Dough will keep a long time.

Creative Play Clay

You Will Need:
 1 cup baking soda
 ½ cup cornstarch
 ⅔ cup warm water
   food coloring or poster paints
   shellac or clear nail polish

How to Make It:
1. Mix baking soda and cornstarch in a saucepan.
2. Add water. Stir until smooth.
3. Place over medium heat and bring to a boil. Cook, stirring constantly, until mixture looks like mashed potatoes.
4. Remove from heat and pour onto mixing board to cool.
5. When dough is cool enough to be easily handled, knead.
6. For color, add food coloring and knead into the dough until well blended or, paint finished, uncolored figures with poster paints.
7. When completely dry, cover figures with shellac or clear nail polish. For figures colored with food coloring, shellac is optional.

Makes about 1½ cups. Double the recipe for large groups or for large objects.

How to Use It: With a rolling pin and cookie cutters or a knife, you can roll and cut out Creative Play Clay to make Christmas tree ornaments, mobiles, and three-dimensional figures.

This mixture can also be molded into almost anything —flowers, animals, birds, and so on. It hardens quickly, so work with only a small amount at a time. The larger the object, the longer it will take to dry.

Stored in plastic bags or in airtight containers, this clay will keep several weeks.

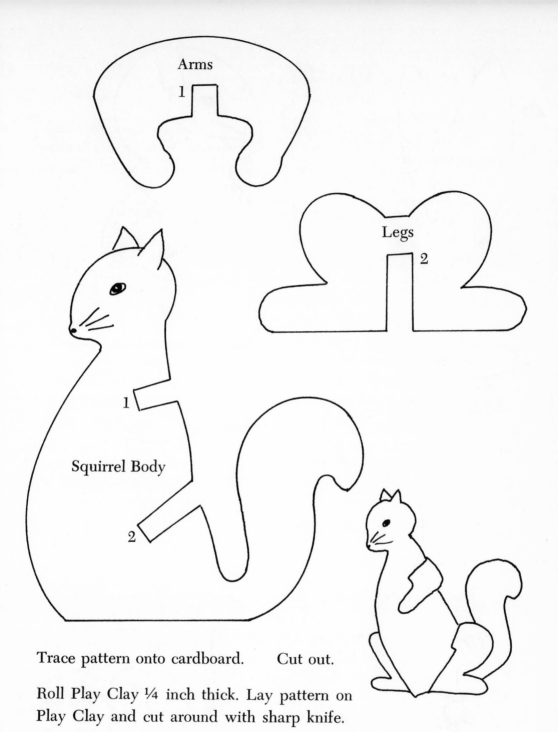

Arms

1

Legs

2

Squirrel Body

1

2

Trace pattern onto cardboard.   Cut out.

Roll Play Clay ¼ inch thick. Lay pattern on Play Clay and cut around with sharp knife.

To assemble, match numbered slots.   Let dry.

Ears or Wings

3

Rabbit Body

3

1

2

Duck Body

3

2

Salt Modeling Clay

You Will Need:
       1 cup non-self-rising wheat flour
     ½ cup salt
       1 teaspoon powdered alum
 ⅓ to ½ cup water
        food coloring (optional)
        model enamel (optional)

How to Make It:
1. Combine flour, salt, and alum in a bowl.
2. Add water a little at a time, and stir into the flour mixture until it is like pie dough.
3. Knead until it is thoroughly mixed and has a smooth consistency.
4. This clay is white. It can be left this way and the finished articles can be painted with model enamel. Or, if desired, food coloring can be added and kneaded into the dough until well blended. The dough can also be divided into portions and a different food coloring can be added to each portion.

Makes about 1½ cups. Double recipe for large groups.

How to Use It: Model as with clay or roll ½ inch thick and cut shapes with a cookie cutter. Make designs by pressing a nail file or similar instrument into the clay. For raised portions, add dough, wetting the underside to make it stick to the basic

piece. This clay is excellent for making Christmas tree ornaments. Glue on a loop of string for hanging.

Within two to three days, Salt Modeling Clay dries to a hard surface. For quick drying, bake on a cookie sheet 1 to 2 hours, depending on the size of the article, at 200 degrees F.

Stored in a plastic bag in an airtight container, this clay will keep a long time.

Sand and Cornstarch Modeling Dough

You Will Need:
 1 cup sand
 ½ cup cornstarch
 1 teaspoon powdered alum
 ¾ cup hot water
    food coloring (optional)

How to Make It:
1. Mix sand, cornstarch, and alum.
2. Add hot water, stirring vigorously until well mixed.
3. Add food coloring, if desired, and blend.
4. Cook over medium heat until thick, stirring constantly.

Makes about 2 cups.

How to Use It: When sufficiently cooled, mold as desired. Dry in the sunshine for several days.

This modeling dough is grainy and stonelike; it can be used to make interesting sculptures. It does not need shellac or varnish to protect it.

Store leftover dough in an airtight container.

Sawdust Modeling Compound

You Will Need:
1 cup fine sawdust
   food coloring (optional)
   old newspaper
1 cup Thin Paste (page 16) or Paper
   Paste (page 17)*
   shellac or clear varnish (optional)

How to Make It:
1. If desired, dye sawdust with food coloring. Drain and spread on newspaper to dry before using.
2. Mix sawdust and paste to a thick dough-like consistency. Knead until thoroughly mixed. The amount of paste may vary according to the kind of sawdust used. If the sawdust is coarse, more paste may be needed to obtain the proper consistency.

Makes about 1 cup.

How to Use It: Model as with clay. Pieces of dough may be added to the basic piece by moistening and sticking them down.

   Within two to three days, the finished article will harden. To speed up drying, bake in a 200-degree-F. oven for 1 to 2 hours, depending on the size of the article.

---

* The amount of paste will vary according to the kind of sawdust used. If the sawdust is coarse, more paste may be needed to obtain the proper consistency.

To give the article a permanent finish, spray with shellac or varnish.

Articles molded from this compound have a lovely wood-grain appearance. They can also be sanded to give a smoother finish.

Soapsuds Clay

You Will Need:
¾ cup soap powder, such as Ivory Snow
1 tablespoon warm water
   electric beater

How to Make It:
1. Mix soap powder and water in a large mixing bowl.
2. Beat with an electric beater to a claylike consistency.

Makes about 1 cup. The recipe may be doubled or tripled for larger objects. Be sure you use the same proportions.

How to Use It: Mold into figures and other objects. The clay dries to a permanently hard finish.

To make simulated snow: Beat 2 parts soap powder to 1 part water and spread like icing on a piece of heavy cardboard. This "icing" may also be used to decorate cardboard Christmas tree ornaments. It dries to a smooth, rubbery surface overnight.

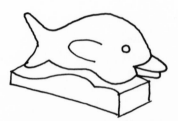

Crepe Paper Clay

You Will Need:
1 cup crepe paper clippings (of one color)
1 cup warm water
½ to ⅔ cup non-self-rising wheat flour

How to Make It:
1. Cut or chop crepe paper into very fine clippings.
2. Place clippings in a bowl and cover with water. Set aside for several hours until soft and pliable.
3. Pour off excess water.
4. Add ½ cup flour and stir until thoroughly mixed.
5. Pour out onto a floured board and knead. Add enough flour to make a pie-crustlike dough.

Makes about 1½ cups.

How to Use It: For jewelry, draw a design on paper and cover with waxed paper. Shape the clay on top of the waxed paper to fit the design underneath. Use a nail or a toothpick for details.

This clay will adhere to glass and can be used to turn jars into vases. It can also be used to sculpt over wire armatures, for mobiles, and so forth.

Crepe Paper Clay dries to a hard finish. It can be sanded to a smooth surface.

Store leftover clay in an airtight container in the refrigerator.

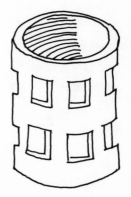

Dryer Lint Modeling Material

You Will Need:
   3 cups of lint (most commercial laundro-
         mats will give you all you want)
   2 cups cold or warm water
   ⅔ cup non-self-rising wheat flour
   3 drops oil of wintergreen
      old newspaper

How to Make It:
1. Put lint and water in a large saucepan. Stir to dampen all parts of the lint.
2. Add flour and stir thoroughly to prevent lumps.
3. Add oil of wintergreen.
4. Cook over low heat, stirring constantly, until mixture holds together and forms peaks.
5. Pour out onto several thicknesses of newspaper to cool.

Makes about 4 cups.

How to Use It: Shape over armatures (boxes, bottles, balloons, and so forth), press into a mold, or use as you would papier-mâché pulp.

   This material will dry in 3 to 5 days to a very hard, durable surface. When wet, it has a feltlike consistency. It dries smooth

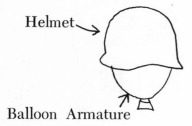

Helmet →

Balloon Armature

or rough, depending on how it is used. When pressed into a mold, a hard, smooth finish is obtained.

Stored in an airtight container, it will keep for several days.

Salt Map Mixture Number One

You Will Need:
  1 part salt
  1 part non-self-rising wheat flour
  ⅔ part water
    food coloring or poster paints
    heavy cardboard

How to Make It:
1. Mix salt and flour until thoroughly blended.
2. Add just enough water to make mixture the consistency of a thick icing. The more water you use, the longer the mixture will take to dry.
3. Stir thoroughly.
4. Add food coloring to mixture before molding, or mold and paint when dry.

How to Use It: Draw map on heavy cardboard. Spread mixture on cardboard, making appropriate hills and valleys. This is also an excellent mixture for making three-dimensional effects such as box dioramas.

This mixture will dry in 1 to 2 days, depending on how thickly it is spread. The longer the mixture takes to dry, the more likely your cardboard is to warp. If only a thin layer of mixture is needed, it will dry quickly and a lighter weight cardboard may be used.

A contour map will keep indefinitely.

Salt Map Mixture Number Two

You Will Need:

2 parts salt

1 part non-self-rising wheat flour

1 part water

food coloring or poster paints

heavy cardboard

How to Make It:

1. Mix salt and flour in a large bowl. The relative amount of each ingredient you use will depend upon the size of your project.

2. Add water a little at a time until the mixture reaches the consistency of icing. Stir thoroughly.

3. Add food coloring to small amounts of the mixture and stir until each color is well blended, or paint the surface with poster paint after it has dried.

How to Use It: Mixture should be used at once. Spread on heavy cardboard as you would do to ice a cake. Build up high elevations a little at a time by allowing the first layer to dry before adding the second layer. It will take 1 to 3 days to dry, depending on the thickness of the mixture.

This mixture has a whiter, grainier texture than Salt Map Mixture Number One (page 51) and dries to a harder surface, but it takes longer to dry. A hardened surface keeps indefinitely.

Bread Dough Clay

You Will Need:
1 slice white bread
1 teaspoon white glue
1 teaspoon water
  food coloring
  clear glaze or clear nail polish

How to Make It:
1. Cut crust from bread.
2. Pour glue, then water, onto the center of the slice of bread.
3. Knead until it doesn't stick to your fingers.
4. Divide dough into several parts and add a few drops of the desired food coloring to each. Knead until color is well blended.
5. Place each color in a separate plastic bag.

Makes enough clay for several small flowers.

How to Use It: Work with only a small portion at a time. Shape your flowers and allow them to dry overnight. When dry, spray with clear glaze or paint with clear nail polish.
    Bread Dough Clay can be stored in the refrigerator for several days.

Styrofoam or Clay

Bread Modeling Dough

You Will Need:
2 slices day-old white bread
2 tablespoons white household glue
2 drops glycerine
4 drops white vinegar
   food coloring or poster paint

How to Make It:
1. Cut or tear crusts from bread.
2. Break bread into small pieces in a bowl.
3. Add glue, glycerine, and vinegar.
4. Mix together with your hands. Knead until it no longer sticks to your fingers and until it is smooth and pliable. (It will be sticky at first, but will soon become pliable and doughlike.)
5. Divide the dough and add a few drops of the desired color to each portion. Knead until the color is smoothly blended.

Makes enough dough for 2 or 3 small objects.

How to Use It: To prevent stickiness when modeling, use hand lotion on your hands. Do not try to make large pieces or the dough will crack when drying.

This dough is excellent for making jewelry, flowers, and doll heads, hands, and feet, and for decorating boxes, frames, and other objects.

Allow to dry 1 to 2 days. Objects made

from this dough dry slowly, but have a smooth satiny finish. A porcelain-like finish can be obtained by painting them with 2 or 3 coats of a mixture of 1 tablespoon of white glue and 1 tablespoon of water. Allow each coat to dry before applying the next. A ceramic-like finish can be obtained by baking the glue-coated objects at 235 degrees F. for 4 minutes.

Stored in plastic bags in the refrigerator, Bread Modeling Dough will keep a long time.

Rose Petal Bead Dough

You Will Need:
⅓ cup non-self-rising wheat flour
 1 tablespoon salt
 2 tablespoons water
 3 cups rose petals
   round toothpicks

How to Make It:
1. Mix flour and salt with water to make a stiff dough.
2. Cut rose petals into tiny pieces, then crush by rolling between your palms.
3. Mix as many rose petals into your dough as possible without making it crumbly.
4. Shape small amounts of dough into beads.
5. Push round toothpicks through the center of each bead to make holes.
6. If desired, scratch rose petal designs into beads.
7. Allow to dry a few days. Remove toothpicks before dough gets too hard.

Makes enough beads for 1 necklace.

How to Use It: String on cord after beads are thoroughly dry.

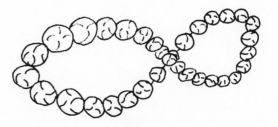

Gesso Modeling Dough

You Will Need:
  1 teaspoon Sobo or other good grade white household glue
  1 tablespoon dextrine solution (1 cup powdered dextrine dissolved in 1 tablespoon hot water)
  ¼ cup plaster of Paris, patching plaster, whiting, Bon Ami, unscented talcum, or powdered chalk
  palette knife or putty knife
  model enamel or tempera and shellac

How to Make It:
1. Pour Sobo onto a plate.
2. Add dextrine solution and mix well.
3. Add plaster of Paris 1 tablespoonful at a time. Mix with a palette knife or putty knife until plaster will not absorb any more solution and can no longer be mixed with knife.
4. Scrape dough together and knead it, using plaster to keep it from sticking to your hands. Knead several minutes, adding more plaster until you have a pliable claylike mixture that is stiff enough to hold its shape.

Makes enough dough for 2 or 3 small objects.

How to Use It: Model small objects such as flowers and ornaments for picture frames, boxes, three-dimensional plaques, and so forth. To fasten pieces together and to a base, mix a few drops of dextrine solution with a few drop of glue and a little plaster.

Set aside to dry for at least a week before painting. To paint, use model enamel or tempera. Apply a coat of shellac over tempera.

Dough made with one of the materials other than plaster may be kept indefinitely if kept moist in an airtight container with a damp cloth. It is best to work with a small amount at a time. Mix a larger amount for larger projects.

Gesso Painting Paste

You Will Need:
1 teaspoon white household glue
1 tablespoon dextrine solution (1 cup powdered dextrine dissolved in 1 tablespoon hot water)
  patching plaster or powdered chalk
  small sharp knife
  oil-paint brush, waxed-paper cone, or cake decorator
  oil paints or enamels

How to Make It:
1. Mix glue with dextrine solution in a small bowl.
2. Add just enough patching plaster to make a paste thick enough to hold its shape but soft enough to brush with an oil-paint brush.

Makes enough gesso for 1 small project.

How to Use It: Draw a pattern or design onto whatever you are decorating (furniture, boxes, beads, picture frames, and so forth) with a pencil. Fill in the design with the gesso until the desired height is attained. This may be done with an oil-paint brush, a waxed-paper cone, or a cake decorator. If you plan

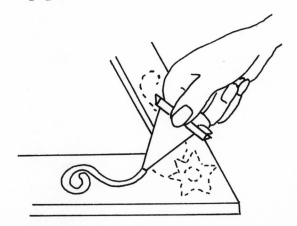

to raise the design to a fairly great height, it is best to raise the whole design only one-third the finished height at a time, allowing each stage to dry before applying the next. The gesso can also be shaped and carved with a small sharp knife to achieve the desired effect.

Gesso is excellent for repairing antique picture frames or furniture. Objects must be free of dirt, grease, or paint. When gesso is dry, paint with oil paints or enamels.

You can also form initials or other designs on waxed paper. When hardened, glue to another surface.

Papier-Máché

Strip Papier-mâché

You Will Need:
a stack of newspapers
Thin Paste (page 16) or Resin Papier-mâché Paste (page 20)

How to Make It:
1. Tear newspapers from the fold down. For large objects, tear the strips 1 to 1½ inches wide. For small objects, tear the strips narrower.
2. If paste is thick, thin it for easy spreading.
3. Lay paper strips on a sheet of newspaper and cover one side of the strips with paste. Strips may also be pulled through paste, but they will take longer to dry. Or paste can be applied to the object and the dry strips laid over the paste.

How to Use It: Strip Papier-mâché is a good material for making small animals, puppets, piñatas, masks, and other articles.

Cover your base or armature (a balloon, a rolled newspaper frame, a jar, a light bulb) with the strips of paste-covered newspaper. Apply a second layer of strips in the same manner, running these strips in the opposite direction. Continue this way until you have built up 4 or 5 layers. To help you determine when you have completely covered the object with each layer, use the colored comic sections for alternate layers.

Allow 1 to 2 days for drying.

Tear from fold down.

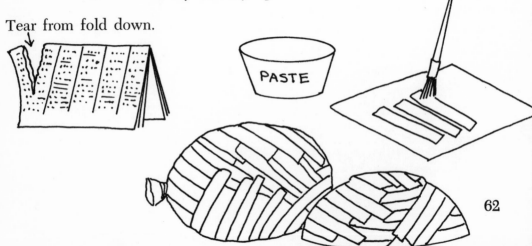

Pasted Paper Layers
Papier-mâché

You Will Need:
old newspaper
Thin Paste (page 16), Paper Paste (page
    17), or Paperhanger's Paste (page 22)
scissors

How to Make It:
1. Cut newspapers into pieces slightly
larger than your intended finished project.
2. Spread a piece of newspaper liberally
with paste and lay a second piece over it.
Cover the second piece with paste and lay
another over it. Continue in this way until
you have built up a strong thick pad.
The number of layers you need will be
determined by the size of the object you
are making. Beginners can start with 6 or
8 layers for small shapes such as jewelry;
add more layers for larger objects.

How to Use It: This papier-mâché is an
excellent material for making flowers.

Draw the outline of your design on the
top sheet and cut it out while the layers
of papier-mâché are still damp. Shape and
set aside for 1 to 2 days to dry.

Very large shapes, such as those used
on parade floats, can also be made if a
layer of cloth is used for strength. Tear
the cloth into the same size as the newspaper pieces. Spread with glue. Use the
cloth as a middle layer; cover with other
newspaper sections.

Basic Papier-mâché Pulp

You Will Need:

1 pail or large pan warm water
1 pail of equal size small torn newspaper pieces
   electric beater
   thick Classroom Paste (page 19), Resin Papier-mâché Paste (page 20), or Wallpaper Paste (page 21)
   oil of wintergreen
   poster paints
   shellac

How to Make It:

1. Tear newspaper into approximately 1-inch-wide strips or into pieces 1 x 1½ inches. (It is up to you which size you decide to use.)

2. Sprinkle strips into water, stirring to separate them until all have been added. If water does not cover, add more until all the paper is covered. Set aside overnight.

3. Beat soaked paper with an electric beater until you have a smooth pulp. If you do not have an electric beater, handfuls of paper can be rubbed over a washboard to achieve the same result, but this takes longer and is more tiresome.

4. Strain out excess water. Squeeze with hands until nearly dry.

5. Add paste gradually. The amount you need depends upon how much paper pulp

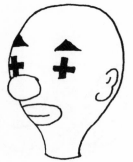

you have and how dry you have squeezed the pulp. Mix to a claylike consistency with an electric beater or with your hands. **6.** Add a few drops of oil of wintergreen to prevent mold while drying.

How to Use It: Mold or model as with clay. Place the object in a spot where the air can circulate around it until it is completely dry. Allow 3 to 5 days to dry, depending on the size of the object. If the object cracks while drying, mend it with additional pulp.

Paint the object with poster paints and then shellac.

Variation: For interesting and different effects, mix sawdust or sand with the pulp. More paste is required in these mixtures.

Salt Papier-mâché

Rolled Newspapers

Newspaper Ball

Plastic Bottle

Tin Can →

← Wire Mesh

Armatures

You Will Need:

a stack of newspaper
water
a large pan or bucket
electric beater
3 parts pulp
1 part non-self-rising wheat flour
⅓ part salt
oil of wintergreen
poster or tempera paints
lacquer or shellac

How to Make It:

1. Tear newspaper into pieces 1 x 1½ inches. Add paper gradually to a large pan or bucket of water, stirring until each piece is wet. Set aside overnight.
2. With an electric beater, beat newspaper pieces to a smooth pulp.
3. Drain excess water and squeeze until just moist. Do not squeeze dry.
4. Mix flour and salt together and add to pulp. With an electric beater, mix until smooth and claylike. If you find you have left too much water, you will need to add more flour.
5. Add a few drops of oil of wintergreen to prevent mold while drying.

How to Use It: Model as with clay or build up object on an armature. Allow 3 to 5 days to dry, depending on the size of the object. Paint with poster or tempera paints. To waterproof the surface, cover with lacquer. If waterproofing is not necessary, cover with shellac.

Large Figure or Float Papier-mâché

You Will Need:
old newspaper
2 gallons warm water
a small tub or 3-gallon pail
electric beater
3 quarts pulp
1 pint paste (any kind)
2 cups plaster of Paris
poster or tempera paints
clear varnish or lacquer

How to Make It:
1. Tear newspaper into long strips.
2. Drop a few strips at a time into the small tub of warm water, stirring to insure that each piece is separated.
3. Set aside overnight.
4. Pour off part of the water and beat the paper pieces to a smooth pulp with an electric beater or with your hands. To mix with your hands, squeeze the mixture through your fingers again and again. Stir up the mixture continually so that all parts become smooth and claylike. Rub stubborn pieces between thumb and fingers to break up.
5. Add paste and plaster of Paris. Beat until smooth and claylike with electric beater or your hands.

Makes enough papier-mâché for 1 fairly large object or several small objects.

How to Use It: Spread mixture over chicken-wire, boxes, or rolled or crumpled newspaper frames. Model as with clay but quickly, for the plaster of Paris makes this papier-mâché set faster and harder than ordinary papier-mâché.

Allow 3 to 5 days to dry thoroughly. Paint with poster or tempera paints. Waterproof with clear varnish or lacquer.

For larger objects, mix more than one batch at a time.

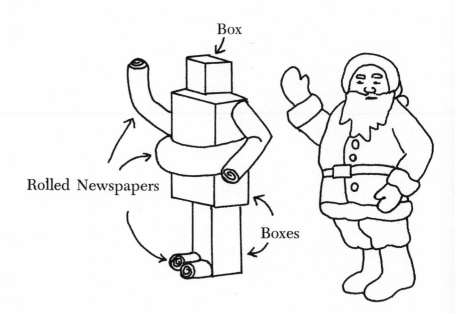

Box

Rolled Newspapers

Boxes

Papier-mâché Mash

You Will Need:
    2-quart bowl or pan
    old newspapers
½ gallon water
1 large enamel or aluminum pot or
      bucket
    slotted spoon
    electric beater
    collander or wire strainer
1 cup non-self-rising wheat flour
4 drops oil of wintergreen
    poster or tempera paints
    shellac or varnish

How to Make It:

1. Fill bowl with newspaper strips torn into pieces ½ x 1½ inches.

2. Place water in large pot and bring to a boil.

3. Add newspaper pieces, a few at a time, to the boiling water, stirring constantly with slotted spoon to separate the pieces.

4. Cook over medium heat about 20 minutes or until the fibers are broken down, stirring occasionally.

5. Beat with electric beater until smooth.

6. Pour into collander to strain out excess water, but do not squeeze.

7. Add flour, mix well, and return strained mixture to heat.

8. Cook at low heat until stiff enough to stand in piles.

9. Add oil of wintergreen and mix.
10. Pour mash onto a thick pad of newspapers to cool.

Makes enough mash for 1 fairly large object or several small objects.

How to Use It: In cooking Papier-mâché Mash, the paper pulp is broken down into a softer, smoother consistency than can be achieved with Basic Papier-mâché Pulp (page 64). The mash dries to a very hard, durable finish. The finished article can be sanded smooth.

Model as with clay. Cover jars and bottles to make candlesticks and vases. To make stools, bookshelves, and end tables, cover each side of a cardboard box with a layer of mash ½ inch thick.

Allow several days to dry. To speed drying, bake at 200 degrees F. The length of time required depends on the size of the article. Check the article frequently to test for dryness.

When dry, sand the article to a smooth finish and paint with poster or tempera paints. Then shellac or varnish.

To make large objects, such as furniture, quadruple the recipe. In place of the 2-quart bowl, a second bucket will be needed.

Stored in the refrigerator, Papier-mâché Mash will keep a long time.

Extra Soft Papier-mâché Pulp

You Will Need:
paper napkins, cleansing tissues, or toilet tissue
Thin Paste (page 16) or white household glue

How to Make It:
1. Crumple napkins or tissue and cover with paste.
2. Model to desired shape.

How to Use It: This pulp is an especially good material for adding such details as noses, ears, eyebrows, and so forth to larger pieces.

It does not keep and must be used immediately.

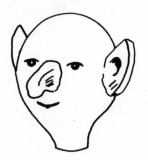

Finishing Touches to Papier-mâché Articles

1. To achieve a harder, more permanent and waterproof surface, use a brush to coat small papier-mâché articles with raw linseed oil. Then bake at 250 degrees F. until dry.

2. To waterproof larger articles, brush on (do not spray) lacquer or clear waterproof varnish.

3. Shellac gives a good permanent finish, but it is not waterproof.

4. Liquid epoxy gives great strength and is flexible, but it should not be used by children working alone.

Casting Compounds

Mock Marble

You Will Need:

2 teaspoons white glue

½ cup water

plaster of Paris

tempera paint (green, blue, gray, or any marble color you prefer)

a mold suitable for plaster casting

How to Make It:

1. Mix glue and water in a medium-sized bowl.

2. Stir in enough plaster of Paris to make a thick frostinglike mixture.

3. Pour the mixture into a shallow soup bowl.

4. Pour a fairly thick coat of tempera paint over the top.

5. Fold in the color to produce streaks. Do not blend.

6. Pour the mixture into a mold.

Plaster of Paris

Spread tempera over top.

Makes about 1 cup. For large molds, double or triple the recipe.

How to Use It: Mock Marble can be used with any plastic or rubber mold suitable for plaster casting. These molds can be purchased at craft or hobby stores.

Mock Marble produces an interesting variation on ordinary plaster of Paris and is more durable.

Imitation Alabaster

Cast figure ← Thread

Can of melted wax →

Pan of hot water →

You Will Need:

2 parts plaster of Paris
1 part water
   a mold suitable for plaster casting
   pure white wax or paraffin
   fine thread or wire

How to Make It:

1. Mix plaster of Paris and water in a bowl. Stir until smooth and creamy.

2. Pour into a mold. Set aside until it hardens.

3. Cut wax into small pieces and put in a tin can. Set can in a pan of hot water over a low flame to melt wax. Wax should be thoroughly melted and hot. Do not omit putting can in a pan of water. It is very dangerous to melt wax over a direct flame.

4. Remove object from mold. Tie a piece of fine thread around object and place it in an approximately 100-degree-F. oven until object becomes warm.

5. Dip warm object into the melted wax. Continue dipping until plaster of Paris absorbs as much wax as possible.

6. Hang article up to dry.

7. Remove thread and polish with a damp cloth.

How to Use It: Imitation Alabaster can be used with any plastic or rubber mold suitable for plaster casting. These molds can be purchased at craft or hobby stores. The plastic bubbles that are used to package hardware items make interesting molds for paperweights or free-art-form statues.

Extra Strong Plaster of Paris
(For Casting)

You Will Need:

2 parts plaster of Paris

1 part water

1 tablespoon white household glue for each ¼ cup water
   a mold suitable for plaster casting

How to Make It:

1. Measure plaster into bowl.

2. Mix water and glue.

3. Pour water and glue mixture into plaster and stir until smooth and creamy. When preparing large amounts, it is better to pour the plaster into the water instead of the water into the plaster.

4. Pour into any plaster-casting mold.

5. Set aside until it hardens. This mixture will dry hard and smooth.

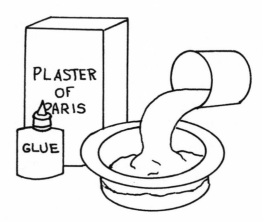

Plaster of Paris Mixture for Dipping Cloth

You Will Need:
1½ parts plaster of Paris
   1 teaspoon powdered alum for each cup water
   1 part water
      cloth, gauze, paper towels, or old sheeting

How to Make It:
1. Mix plaster of Paris and alum.
2. Add plaster and alum mixture to water.
3. Stir until smooth and creamy.

How to Use It: Dip cloth into plaster mixture. Model the cloth over a bottle, a cardboard cone, wire, or whatever you are using for an armature. You will have 15 to 20 minutes to drape and shape the cloth before it dries. It will dry very hard.

Slow Drying
Dipping Mixture

You Will Need:
- 1 gallon milk carton for mixing
- 1½ cups water
- 1 cup spackle compound
- 1 cup plaster of Paris
- 1 teaspoon powdered alum
  - slotted spoon
  - poster paint if desired
  - cloth, gauze, paper towels, or old sheeting

How to Make It:
1. Cut top off milk carton. Pour water into carton.
2. Mix spackle, plaster of Paris, and alum together.
3. Sprinkle into water, allowing it to pile up in the center.
4. Stir with a slotted spoon until smooth and creamy.
5. Add poster paint if desired.

How to Use It: Dip cloth into mixture, then drape and shape it around a bottle, armature, or other object as desired. Since this mixture requires 45 minutes to set, you have plenty of time to mold or to correct mistakes.

It is a good mixture to use for making large parade float figures over a base of chicken wire.

The recipe can be doubled, but for large objects it is better to mix 2 smaller amounts rather than 1 large amount to prevent the mixture from setting before you have finished.

Paints and Paint Mediums

A paint medium is any liquid, such as oil or water, with which pigment is mixed in preparing it for application. In this section you will find several recipes for paints and paint mediums.

Finger Paint
Number One

You Will Need:
½ cup non-self-rising wheat flour
2 cups water
1 tablespoon glycerine
1 teaspoon borax for preservative
   small screw-top jars
   food coloring or poster paints

How to Make It:
1. Mix flour with ½ cup of water to form a paste.
2. Add the rest of the water and cook over low heat until thick and clear, stirring constantly.
3. Cool. Add glycerine and borax. If mixture is too thick and does not spread easily, thin with a small amount of water.
4. Divide and pour into small screw-top jars, such as baby food jars. Add food coloring or poster paints to color.

Makes about 2 cups. For a large group of children, double the recipe.

How to Use It: Dip shelf paper or typing paper into water and spread smoothly on a Formica tabletop or on newspapers. Add a dab of finger paint and make a picture or a design. To make finger paint spread evenly, dip your hands in water.

This finger paint spreads easily and thinly. It is flexible and does not crack or peel from paper when it is folded. It works as well on dry paper as it does on wet paper. With dry paper there is less curl.

Stored in airtight containers, this finger paint will keep a long time.

Finger Paint
Number Two

You Will Need:
½ cup cornstarch
¾ cup cold water
2 cups hot water
2 teaspoons boric acid solution for preservative
1 tablespoon glycerine
  small screw-top jars
  food coloring or poster paints

How to Make It:
1. Mix cornstarch with ¼ cup of cold water to make a smooth paste.
2. Add hot water, stirring vigorously to prevent lumps.
3. Cook over low heat, stirring constantly, until mixture begins to boil.
4. Remove from heat and add ½ cup cold water and boric acid solution. Stir until thoroughly mixed.
5. Add glycerine to mixture to slow up drying process.
6. Divide into separate screw-top jars and add food coloring or poster paints for color. Stir until color is completely blended.

Makes about 2½ cups. For a large group of children, double the recipe.

How to Use It: Because it dries slowly, this is an excellent finger paint to use with small children. It has a smoother, glossier finish and is more transparent than Finger Paint Number One (page 80). It works as well on dry paper, which will have less curl, as it does on wet paper.

Stored in airtight containers, this finger paint will keep a long time.

Finger Paint
Number Three

You Will Need:

¼ cup laundry starch
¼ cup cold water
1½ cups boiling water
2 tablespoons talcum powder, prefer-
   ably unscented
¼ cup soap powder, such as Ivory Snow
½ teaspoon boric acid solution
4 small screw-top jars
1 tablespoon poster paint to each drop
   of base or ¾ tablespoon powdered
   tempera or several drops food
   coloring.

How to Make It:

1. Mix starch with cold water to make a smooth paste.
2. Add boiling water, stirring vigorously to prevent lumps.
3. Cook over low heat until clear and thick, stirring constantly.
4. Remove from stove and add talcum powder. Stir until blended.
5. Add soap powder and boric acid solution. Mix until thoroughly blended.
6. Pour into four ½-cup screw-top jars (baby food jars are ideal).
7. Add 1½ teaspoons of poster paint to each jar. Allow to cool.

Makes 2 cups. For large groups, double the recipe.

How to Use It: This paint is thick and works best on wet paper. It has a flat finish and is more opaque than Finger Paint Number One (page 80) and Number Two (page 82).

In tightly capped jars, this paint can be stored for a long time.

Finger Paint
Number Four

You Will Need:
½ cup cornstarch
¾ cup cold water
1 envelope of unflavored gelatin
¼ cup cold water
2 cups boiling water
  small screw-top jars
  food coloring or poster paints

How to Make It:
1. Mix cornstarch with ¾ cup of water to a smooth paste in a saucepan.
2. Soak gelatin in ¼ cup of cold water. Set aside until ready to use.
3. Pour boiling water slowly into the cornstarch mixture, stirring as you pour.
4. Cook over medium heat, stirring constantly, until mixture boils and is clear.
5. Remove from heat. Stir in gelatin.
6. Cool and divide into different jars for various colors. Stir food coloring or poster paint into each jar until well blended.

Makes about 2½ cups.

How to Use It: This paint is transparent and has a strong, durable, high-gloss finish. Use it on wet or dry paper. It is excellent paint for covering boxes, scrapbooks, and so on. It dries more quickly than Finger Paint Number Two (page 82).

If refrigerated, it will keep a few days.

Sealing Wax Paint

You Will Need:
sticks of leftover bits of sealing wax of
  various colors
lemon or peppermint extract, or denatured
  alcohol
airtight jar for each color

How to Make It:
1. Crush each stick of sealing wax into
small bits and place them in a small airtight jar (one for each color of sealing
wax).
2. Cover wax with the extract or the alcohol. Set aside for at least 24 hours or until
wax dissolves completely.
3. Shake well before using. If too thick,
add more extract, or alcohol. If too thin,
set aside for a while without lid.

How to Use It: Use this paint as you
would use oil paint or dilute with extract
or alcohol and use as a wash. Sealing Wax
Paint can be painted over oils, or use it on
paper or to decorate cork, wood, beads,
picture frames, or almost anything.

   Clean your brushes with extract or alcohol.
   This paint will keep forever. If it dries
out, add extract.

Simple Egg
Tempera Emulsion

Egg Mixture

You Will Need:
2 measures of egg yolk
1 measure of water
   assorted powdered pigments or poster colors
   palette pan

How to Make It:
1. Since egg yolks vary in size, place the egg yolks in a measuring cup and break the yolks. Then determine the amount of measures of egg yolk to determine the amount of water you will need. The relation is 2 to 1. For example, if you have 2 tablespoons of egg yolk, you will need 1 tablespoon of water.
2. Mix egg yolks and water thoroughly until well blended. Do not beat.
3. Mix a small amount of the egg mixture with each powdered pigment. Work with brush in a palette pan until thoroughly mixed.

Two egg yolks make about ¼ cup. For large groups, mix any amount of eggs to half as much water.

How to Use It: This emulsion is a permanent paint with an opaque finish. One color can be painted over another. Mix only as much pigment as you will be using at one time.

   It is water soluble. Use water to thin and to clean brushes.

   Stored in an airtight jar in the refrigerator, the base emulsion will keep for several days.

Egg Tempera Emulsion

You Will Need:
 1 tablespoon dammar varnish (purchased at art supply or craft stores)
   an 8-ounce bottle or jar
 1 whole medium-sized egg
 1 tablespoon raw linseed oil
3–4 tablespoons water (depending on
   how thick or thin you want your
   solution)
   powdered pigments

How to Make It:
1. Pour a small amount of dammar varnish into a clean bottle. Shake to coat all sides; pour out any remaining varnish.
2. Break the egg into the bottle and shake until the yolk and the white are thoroughly mixed.
3. Add linseed oil and 1 tablespoon dammar varnish and shake again until thoroughly blended.
4. Add the water and shake again until well blended.

Makes about ½ cup.

How to Use It: Mix this emulsion with powdered pigments when you are ready to use it. Use water or base emulsion to thin. It dries waterproof with a mat finish.

Egg Tempera Emulsion is more brittle

than oils and has a tendency to crack when applied in thick layers. When this emulsion is used on canvas, panel, or good watercolor paper, attractive paintings can be produced.

Clean brushes immediately with soap and water.

Store base emulsion in a tightly capped jar in the refrigerator.

Old-Fashioned Gouache Paint Medium

You Will Need:

5 ounces of gum arabic (if you can get it) or gum tragacanth

½ cup distilled water

a pint jar

½ cup honey

1 tablespoon glycerine

½ tablespoon boric acid solution

powdered pigment or poster paints

How to Make It:

1. Dissolve the gum arabic in water in a pint jar.

2. Mix in honey, glycerine, and boric acid solution.

3. Stir or shake until thoroughly blended.

Makes about 1½ cups.

How to Use It: Mix this gouache base with powdered pigments or poster paints in a palette pan when you are ready to use it. Muffin tins make good pans for mixing pigments with gouache.

Gouache, which is opaque, can be used on illustration board or heavy drawing paper as you would use oil paints.

Zinc oxide mixed with gouache base makes a good white pigment.

Gouache is an interesting medium to

work with and makes an inexpensive base for teaching young beginning painters. It has the advantage of being water soluble so that clean-up time is easier. Use water to thin gouache and to clean your brushes.

Stored in an airtight jar, gouache will keep for several months.

Gouache Paint Medium

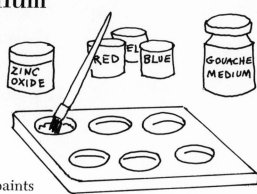

You Will Need:
- 2 cups dextrine
  - a pint jar
- 4 tablespoons distilled water
- ½ cup honey
- 2 teaspoons glycerine
- ½ teaspoon boric acid solution
  - powdered pigments or poster paints

How to Make It:
1. Pour dextrine into a pint jar.
2. Add water and stir until dextrine is dissolved. The saccharin in the dextrine will cause the mixture to foam; this does not matter.
3. Add honey, glycerine, and boric acid solution.
4. Stir or shake until all ingredients are well blended.

Makes about ¾ cup.

How to Use It: Mix this gouache base with powdered pigments or poster paints when you are ready to use it. It is opaque and dries rapidly. One color can be painted over another. This gouache medium is a good substitute for Old-Fashioned Gouache Paint Medium (page 91) if you cannot obtain gum arabic.

Use water to thin medium and to clean your brushes.

Stored in a tightly capped jar, Gouache Paint Medium will keep for a long time.

Gouache Paint

You Will Need:
  2 cups dextrine
       a pint jar
  4 tablespoons distilled water
  2 tablespoons glycerine
  ½ teaspoon boric acid solution
       powdered pigments
       zinc oxide
       a flat plate
       a palette knife
       small screw-top jars

How to Make It:

GOUACHE BASE

1. Pour dextrine into a pint jar. Add distilled water and stir until dextrine is completely dissolved. The saccharin in the dextrine will cause the mixture to foam; this does not matter.
2. Add glycerine and boric acid solution.
3. Put lid on jar and shake until thoroughly blended.

Makes slightly more than ½ cup.

GOUACHE PAINT

1. Pour 1 or 2 tablespoons of one powdered pigment and an equal amount of

zinc oxide into a flat plate. Mix thoroughly with a palette knife.

2. Add enough gouache base to make paint a soft butterlike consistency. Mix thoroughly with palette knife until smooth.

3. Lift paint with palette knife and transfer to screw-top jars.

How to Use It: Gouache Paint is opaque, dries rapidly, is water soluble, and has a flat finish. It will become a darker color when it dries. Use it on paper, poster board, illustration board, or anything you would use with watercolors. Mix larger amounts for painting large objects, such as stage backdrops.

Clean your brushes with water.

Gouache Paint can be thinned with water or with uncolored gouache base.

Stored in a tightly capped jar, this paint will keep for several weeks.

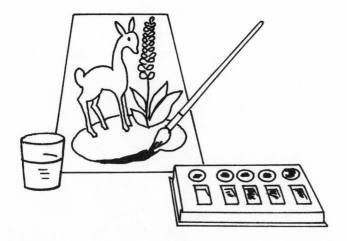

Mucilage Gouache Paint Medium

You Will Need:
½ cup gum mucilage
½ cup strained honey
   a ½-pint jar
      powdered pigments or poster paints
      zinc oxide, if desired (see Helpful
         Hints, Number 2)

How to Make It:
1. Mix mucilage and honey together in a ½-pint jar.
2. Shake until smoothly blended.

Makes about 1 cup.

How to Use It: Mix this medium with powdered pigments or poster paints when you are ready to use it. Use zinc powder for white pigment. This is a simple solution to mix, but it dries slowly.

Use water to thin medium and to clean your brushes.

Stored in a tightly capped jar, this medium will keep for several months.

Casein Paint Medium

You Will Need:
  2 tablespoons borax
  ½ cup warm water
  ¼ cup powdered nonfat milk
      powdered pigments

How to Make It:
1. Dissolve borax in warm water.
2. Add powdered milk. Stir until completely blended. Mixture should be a thick, creamy solution.

Makes about ¾ cup.

How to Use It: Combine only as much medium with colors as you intend to use at one sitting. Using a brush, mix a small amount of the medium with powdered pigments in a palette pan until it is the consistency of thick cream.

    Casein Paint Medium dries quickly to a semigloss finish. One color can be painted over another.

    Use water to thin medium and to clean your brushes.

    Stored in a screw-top jar in the refrigerator, this medium will keep several weeks.

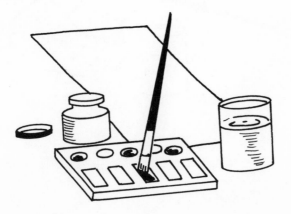

Casein Paint

You Will Need:
2 parts casein glue (white household glue)
1 part water
   powdered pigment, poster paints, or opaque watercolor

How to Make It:
1. Mix glue and water.
2. Add mixture to powdered pigment. Mix until paint is the consistency of thick cream.

How to Use It: Casein Paint, which has a flat finish, is especially good for painting waxed surfaces such as milk cartons and cottage cheese cartons. When you want a more permanent finish than can be obtained with tempera or poster paints, use Casein Paint.
   Use water to thin paint and to clean your brushes.
   Store this paint in a tightly capped jar.

Powdered Milk Paint Medium

You Will Need:
½ cup powdered nonfat milk
½ cup water
   powdered paint pigments

How to Make It:
1. Mix milk and water. Stir until milk is dissolved.
2. Combine only as much solution with powdered pigments as you intend to use at one sitting.

Makes about ¾ cup. For a large group, combine any amount of powdered milk with an equal amount of water.

How to Use It: Mix a small amount of the solution with powdered pigment in a palette pan. Work smooth with a brush.

   This paint dries quickly to a glossy, opaque finish. It does not dust, chip, or come off on your hands the way poster paint does.

   Use water to thin paint and to clean your brushes.

   Store this medium in a tightly capped jar in the refrigerator.

Frescoes

You Will Need:
a wooden picture frame (a narrow frame is preferable)
a piece of ⅛-inch plywood to fit inside the frame (any thin
  board may be used)
plaster (patching plaster can be used)
water
paints that won't be injured by lime in the plaster (watercolors,
  poster paints, or tempera)
cardboard, hammer, and tacks

How to Make It:
1. Cut the plywood to fit inside the back of the frame. Tack in
place.
2. Mix plaster according to instructions on package, pour out
and cover the board on the frame side with about ¼ inch of
plaster.
3. Use the edge of a piece of cardboard cut to the width of the
frame to smooth the surface. Gently tap to remove all bubbles.
4. Let plaster set until almost dry but still damp.

How to Use It: While plaster is still damp, paint a design or
picture on it. Use either free-hand or stencil designs. As the
plaster continues to dry, the pigment sets in the plaster.

  To determine if paint is limeproof, mix a small amount of the
paint with dry plaster. After a week or so, if no change takes
place in the color, the paint can be used.

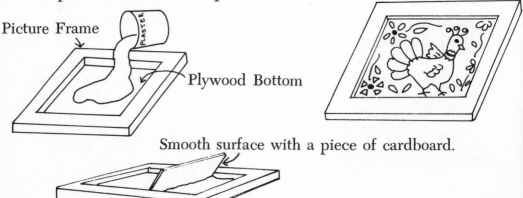

Picture Frame

Plywood Bottom

Smooth surface with a piece of cardboard.

Marbleizing

You Will Need:
8 packets (2 ounces) unflavored gelatin
1 pint boiling water
    shallow baking pan
5 pints cold water
    oil paints
    turpentine
    brown wrapping paper or paper bags

How to Make It:
1. Dissolve gelatin in boiling water.
2. Pour mixture into shallow pan and add cold water.
3. Mix oil paints with a bit of turpentine to the consistency of thick cream.
4. Drop a few drops of color into solution in shallow pan. If the color sinks, it is too thick. If it spreads too much, it is too thin. When just right, drop large spots of color, one at a time, into the solution.
5. With a spoon or stick, swirl into patterns.

How to Use It: Cut a piece of brown paper to the size of the pan. Hold the paper by opposite corners and lower onto the solution. Lift paper carefully and lay right side up on a stack of newspaper to dry.

Marbelized paper can be used for covering scrapbooks, notebooks, lampshades, wastebaskets, and many other objects.

Clean pan with turpentine.

Inks

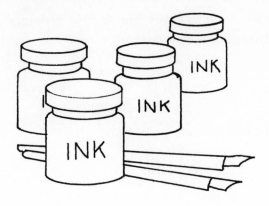

Transfer Ink

You Will Need:
  2 tablespoons soap powder, such as Ivory Snow (not a deter-
      gent) or scrapings from a bar of soap
  ¼ cup hot water
  1 tablespoon turpentine

How to Make It:
1. Dissolve soap powder in hot water.
2. Add turpentine.
3. When cool, pour into a screw-top bottle.

Makes about ¾ cup.

How to Use It: Dip a watercolor brush into the ink and brush
over the picture to be transferred. Wait about 10 seconds.
Place a piece of paper over the picture and rub the back of it
with a spoon. The picture will soon be transferred to the paper.

You can transfer an entire picture or just a portion of it by
inking only the part you wish to transfer. Comic strip characters
transfer especially well. Magazine pictures will also transfer,
but slick papers require a bit more ink. One picture can usually
be used more than once.

You can use Transfer Ink to make stationery, greeting cards,
and composite pictures. You can take a picture from a magazine
for a school report, transfer wallpaper designs onto lampshades
or designs onto shirts. The possibilities are unlimited.

Transfer Ink may be stored indefinitely without refrigeration.
If the ink solidifies, set the bottle in a pan of warm water until
the ink becomes liquid again. Shake well before using.

Rubber Stamp Ink

You Will Need:
   powdered clothes dye, any color
¼ teaspoon alcohol
 5 tablespoons glycerine

How to Make It:
1. Mix dye with alcohol to the consistency of thin cream.
2. Add glycerine. Stir until well blended.

Makes enough ink to replenish stamp pad several times.

How to Use It: Pour ink over stamp pad or over a fine-grained foam-rubber pad.

   To make a stamp pad, cut foam rubber to fit the bottom of a small plastic box. Pour Rubber Stamp Ink over the pad and spread evenly with a brush or a tongue depressor. When not in use, keep the box tightly covered. This ink is waterproof.

Foam Rubber —   ← Plastic Pin Box

Block Printing Ink

You Will Need:
3 tablespoons powdered pigment
1 tablespoon clear varnish
   palette knife
   sheet of glass
   brayer

How to Make It:
1. Mix pigment and varnish thoroughly with a palette knife on a glass surface.
2. Roll brayer back and forth until the mixture is tacky and the brayer is evenly coated.

Makes enough ink for 1 project. For large groups, double or triple the recipe.

How to Use It: When the brayer is evenly coated, roll it over a carved wood or linoleum block. Press the block on paper and apply weight evenly.
   To make potato or spool prints, press a carved potato or spool into the ink on the glass and then print on paper.

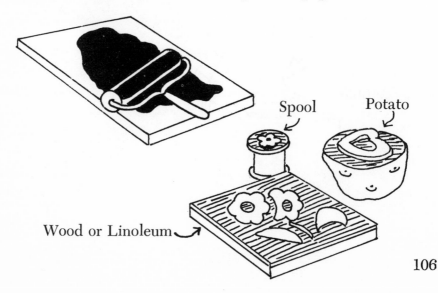

Spool   Potato

Wood or Linoleum

106

Block Printing Ink for Fabric

You Will Need:

5 tablespoons turpentine
2 tablespoons vinegar
1 tablespoon oil of wintergreen
1 tablespoon Ivory dishwashing liquid
  an 8-ounce bottle
  oil paint pigments
  palette knife
  sheet of glass
  brayer
  carved wood or linoleum block
  a piece of fabric
  a hot iron

How to Make It:

1. Pour first 4 ingredients into bottle and shake well.
2. Thin oil paint pigments with this solution to the consistency of thick cream. Work smooth with a palette knife on a sheet of glass.
3. Roll brayer back and forth until mixture is tacky and the brayer is evenly coated.

Makes enough ink for 1 project.

How to Use It: When brayer is evenly coated, roll it over the carved block. Press the block over the fabric and apply weight evenly. Remove the block from the fabric and place a damp cloth over the designed fabric. Press the designed fabric with a hot iron.

The designed fabric can be washed in warm water with a mild soap.

Waterproof Ink

You Will Need:
1 tablespoon powdered clothes dye
   (more may be added for deeper
   color)
2 teaspoons peppermint extract
1 tablespoon glycerine
¾ cup distilled water

How to Make It:
1. Dissolve dye in extract.
2. Mix with glycerine.
3. Dissolve mixture in distilled water.

Makes about ¾ cup.

How to Use It: Waterproof Ink can be
used to stencil or paint fabrics, to make
laundry marks, and so on.
   Store this ink in a screw-top bottle.

Hectograph Ink

You Will Need:

1½ teaspoons water-based pigment, such as Prussian blue, iodine-green, methyl violet, and so on. (Do not use an oil paint pigment. Aniline dye is best but poisonous.)

1 teaspoon glycerine

4 teaspoons distilled water

⅔ teaspoon peppermint or lemon extract

How to Make It:

1. Mix the pigment with glycerine until smooth and well blended.

2. Add water and extract. Stir or shake until thoroughly mixed.

Makes about 2 tablespoons—enough for several projects.

How to Use It: Store in a tightly capped bottle. Shake bottle well before using. Draw or write with a lettering pen or a fine brush on typing paper. Make reprints on a hectograph pad, a kind of duplicator with a gelatin pad. You can make one (page 110) or buy one.

Hectograph Pad

You Will Need:
2 cups water
4 packets (1 ounce) unflavored gelatin
   a baking pan, 8 x 11 inches
2 teaspoons boric acid solution

How to Make It:
1. Pour water over gelatin and let stand for 2 to 3 hours.
2. Pour softened gelatin into baking pan.
3. Slowly bring to a boil, then reduce heat and let simmer over a low flame for 20 minutes. Add boric acid solution.
4. Set aside overnight.

How to Use It: A Hectograph Pad is used to make duplicate copies of letters or pictures. First write a letter or draw on typing or similar paper with Hectograph Ink (page 109), hectograph pencils or copy pencils. Gently sponge the surface of the gelatin pad. The pad should be wet, but there should not be any puddles of water. Place the letter or drawing on the pad, face down, and rub out all wrinkles. Wait one minute, then remove the master sheet. You can now make copies from the pad. Lay clean sheets of paper, one at a time, over the drawing. Smooth it by rubbing out wrinkles. Remove immediately. You can make as many copies as you want in this manner. When you are finished, wash the pad with a sponge and cold water. When dry, it will be ready for reuse.

   If the pad dries out from lack of use, cover the top of the gelatin with warm water. Let stand for a few minutes, or until it no longer feels dry when sponged.

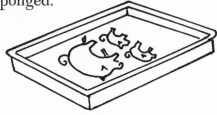

Dried Flower Preservatives

Flower Preservative with Cornmeal

You Will Need:
1 part powdered borax
2 parts cornmeal
  covered cardboard box (a shoe box or stationary box)
  fresh flowers

How to Make It:
1. Thoroughly mix borax and cornmeal.
2. Cover the bottom of the box with ¾ of an inch of this mixture.
3. Cut flower stems about 1 inch long. Lay the flowers face down in this mixture. Spread the petals and leaves so that they lie as flat as possible. Do not place flowers too close together.
4. Cover the flowers with ¾ of an inch of mixture.
5. Place lid on box and keep at room temperature for 3 to 4 weeks.

How to Use It: Try daisies, pansies, apple blossoms, asters, violets, and other flowers with this method. They will stay summer fresh indefinitely. This is an excellent way to preserve corsages or flowers from someone special.

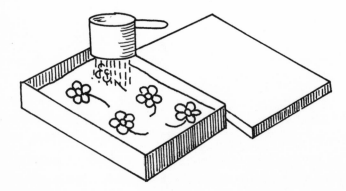

Flower Preservative with Borax

You Will Need:
fresh flowers (roses, pansies, violets, sweet peas, chrysanthe-
   mums, zinnias, marigolds, and daisies)
florist's wire
airtight container (coffee can or plastic cheese container)
plastic bag
borax
wire or string
soft brush

How to Make It:
1. Pick flowers at the peak of their bloom.
2. Remove stems. Make new stems with florist's wire. Run wire
through the base of the flower and twist the two ends together.
3. Line the coffee can or plastic cheese container with the
plastic bag.
4. Pour enough borax into the plastic bag to cover the bottom
to a depth of 1 inch.
5. Place flower face down in the borax. Pour about 1 inch of
borax over the top of the flower. Add more flowers and borax
until the container is full.
6. Gather the top of the bag, squeezing out all the air inside it.
Fasten shut with wire or string.
7. Place lid on can and set aside in a dry place for at least 4
weeks.
8. Remove flowers from borax and carefully brush away all
borax with a soft brush.

How to Use It: Using the wire stems, make an attractive flower
arrangement as you would a fresh-flower bouquet. Flowers
preserved in this way make colorful permanent floral arrangements. Flowers picked at the peak of their bloom remain fresh
looking indefinitely.

113

Flower Preservative
with Sand

You Will Need:
a baking pan, 9½ x 13½ x 2 inches
3 quarts of sterile, dry, fine sand (fine
white sand can be purchased, but any
clean light-colored sand can be used if
it is first sifted through a fine screen)
fresh flowers
flour sifter or wire sieve
soft brush

How to Make It:
1. Fill the pan 1 inch deep with sand.
2. Place flowers face up on the sand.
3. Sift about 1 inch of sand over the
flowers, carefully pushing sand under
flowers so that they do not dry distorted.
4. Bake at 200 degrees F. for about 2
hours. You might need to experiment a
little to get the exact time for your flowers.
To test, pour a little sand off one corner. If
the flowers are still damp and droopy,
they need to bake a little longer. If they
are dull and dark, they baked too long.
They should look about the same as they
did when you put them in.
5. Carefully remove the flowers from the
sand by pouring off the top layer. Lay
them on a paper to cool for an hour or so.

6. Carefully clean off all the sand that remains on the flowers with a soft brush.

How to Use It: Flowers preserved by this method are excellent for picture arrangements. Glue them to velvet or cardboard and then frame the picture.

To store flowers until you are ready to use them in a project, place them face down in cardboard boxes. The flowers will stay fresh-looking for a long time.

Miscellaneous

Fixative

You Will Need:
1 part pure white shellac
  a screw-top glass jar
1 part denatured alcohol
  an atomizer or spray gun

How to Make It:
1. Pour shellac into jar.
2. Add alcohol.
3. Screw cap on tightly and shake until well blended.
4. Pour fixative into an atomizer or spray gun.

How to Use It: To prevent charcoal, chalk, pastel, and pencil drawings from smudg- ing, spray fixative on artwork from a distance of about 20 inches.

Crayon Cloth Design

You Will Need:
 cloth
 crayons
 iron
 drawing board
 thumbtacks
 newspapers
½ cup vinegar
 1 cup water
 cloth for pressing
 3 tablespoons salt
 1 quart water

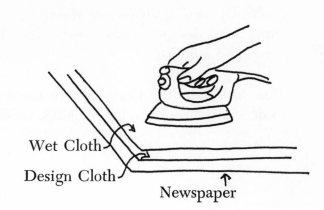

Wet Cloth

Design Cloth

Newspaper

How to Do It:

1. Wash cloth to remove all sizing (stiffeners) from the fabric.

2. Stencil, draw or transfer, design directly onto the cloth.

 To make a transfer pattern, draw a design on lightweight paper, then outline it with a sharp-pointed red or orange crayon. Lay the paper design face down on the cloth. Run a medium hot iron over the back of the paper to transfer the design onto the cloth.

3. Stretch the cloth smoothly and tightly over the drawing board. Thumbtack securely in place.

4. Color in your design with crayons, using an even, regular stroke. The more crayon you add, the deeper the color will be.

5. Remove cloth from drawing board. Turn the color design face down on several sheets of newspaper.

6. Mix vinegar and 1 cup water. Dip pressing cloth into vinegar mixture and squeeze out most of the fluid. Place the

pressing cloth over the designed cloth and press with a hot iron.
7. Mix salt and 1 quart water. Soak the designed cloth in this solution for 3 to 4 hours.
8. Gently wash in lukewarm water and mild soap. After it has dried, your design is permanent. It can be laundered in warm water and mild soap.

How to Use It: The Crayon Cloth Design method can be used to decorate dishcloths, lunch cloths, curtains, and so on.

Gesso Ground for Scratchboard

You Will Need:
1 part glue water (1 ounce gelatin to 16 ounces hot water)
1 part zinc white
1 part plaster of Paris
    illustration board

How to Make It:
1. Mix gelatin and water to make glue water. Set aside to cool.
2. Mix glue water with zinc white and plaster of Paris.
3. Stir until completely smooth and free from all grains.
4. Paint onto illustration board.
5. Dry overnight.

How to Use It: Paint over gesso ground with paint or black ink.
Scratch a design or picture in the painted gesso with a needle,
a nail, or other sharp instrument.

   This gesso cannot be stored. Mix only as much as you will
need for one project.

Scratch in design.

India Ink

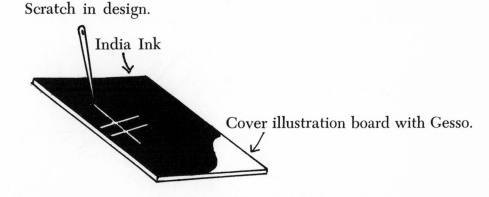

Cover illustration board with Gesso.

Crepe Paper Raffia

You Will Need:

strips of crepe paper, 2 to 3 inches wide (use crepe paper
    streamers or cut streamers from the end of a package)
a spool or a thumbtack and a hand drill
clear spray varnish or shellac

How to Make It:
1. Thread one end of the crepe paper through the hole in the
spool.
2. Twist and pull the entire length of crepe paper through the
spool.
   Or:
1. Fasten down one end of crepe paper with a thumbtack.
2. Fasten the other end to a hand drill.
3. Twist until paper is firm and cordlike.

How to Use It: One strip of raffia will be more than enough to
cover a juice can, which you can use as a pencil holder. Wrap
other containers in raffia to make attractive wastebaskets, sew-
ing baskets, May baskets, and so on.
   Coat the finished product with clear spray varnish or shellac.

Spool

Cut

←2-3"→

CREPE PAPER

Colored Flame Solution

You Will Need:

1½ pounds rock salt

½ gallon water

2 pounds of one of the following chemicals: calcium chloride (orange flame), potassium chloride (purple), copper chloride (blue), strontium nitrate (red), copper sulphate (emerald green), or lithium chloride (carmine)

a small plastic tub or dishpan

stacks of old newspapers, pine cones or wood chips

heavy string

How to Make It:

1. Mix salt, water, and one of the chemicals in the plastic tub.

2. Fold several sheets of newspaper in half and roll into compact logs.

3. Tie logs securely with heavy string, but not too tightly because they will swell when they soak.

4. Soak the logs in the chemical solution for 3 weeks. Turn them frequently.

5. Remove logs from solution and dry completely before burning. This can take a week or more, depending upon how damp the air is.

To treat pine cones or wood chips:

1. Place cones or chips in a mesh bag, such as a plastic onion or potato bag.

2. Mix 1 pound of a chemical in 1 gallon of water in a plastic bucket.

3. Submerge the bag of cones or chips in the solution and weight it down with a brick or stone to prevent it from floating.

4. Soak for 10 to 15 minutes.

5. Pour out onto newspaper to dry over-night.

How to Use It: When you burn these "logs" in your fireplace, each chemical produces a different colored flame.

Double or triple the recipe to make large quantities of logs.

Crystal Garden Solution

You Will Need:

    a few pieces of coal or some rocks
    a shallow bowl
6 tablespoons salt
6 tablespoons bluing
6 tablespoons water
1 tablespoon ammonia
    food coloring

How to Make It:

1. Place the coal or rocks in the bottom of the shallow bowl.

2. Combine salt, bluing, water, and ammonia in a small bowl and mix well.

3. Pour mixture over coal or rocks.

4. Add a few drops of different food coloring over the mixture.

5. Let stand a few hours. Crystals will begin to form. They will grow to be colorful and interesting for several days.

Stenciling Paper

You Will Need:
shirt cardboard
candle or tallow
iron

How to Make It:
1. Rub shirt or similar weight cardboard with candle or tallow.
2. Iron with moderately warm iron to melt candle wax into cardboard.
3. Allow to cool.

How to Use It: When your stencil paper is completely cool it is ready to use. Draw your design on the paper and cut it out with mat knife or single-edge razor blade.

Candle

Shirt Cardboard

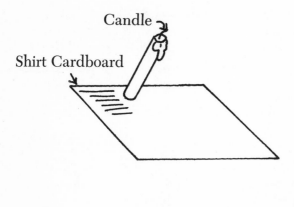

Index